Nothing Vanishes

Nothing Vanishes

Robert Hilles

Wolsak and Wynn . Toronto

Typeset in Times Roman, printed in Canada on Zephir Laid by The Coach House Printing Company, Toronto

Cover design: Tivador Bote
Author's photo: Shelley Sopher

Many of the pieces here have appeared in various publications. I wish to thank the editors of the following publications for their editorial suggestions and faith: *Descant, Capilano Review, Event, Raffia, Prairie Journal of Canadian Literature, Blue Buffalo, Dandelion, Quarry, Prairie Fire, Sanscrit, West Coast Line, Canadian Forum, White Wall Review, NeWest Review,* and the anthology *A Discord of Flags.* Mick Burrs has given much time and thought to editing the individual poems in this book; the author thanks him sincerely for his valuable help.

The publishers gratefully acknowledge support from The Canada Council and The Ontario Arts Council which has made publication of this book possible.

Wolsak and Wynn Publishers Ltd.
Don Mills Post Office Box 316
Don Mills, Ontario, Canada, M3C 2S7

Canadian Cataloguing in Publication Data

Hilles, Robert, 1951-
  Nothing Vanishes
Poems.

ISBN 0-919897-52-5
I. Title.
PS8565.I48N6 1996   C811'.54   C96-931121-4
PR9199.3.H55N6 1996

For Rebecca, Breanne, and Austin
with a special thanks to Mick Burrs
for his careful editing of each poem

CONTENTS

Blue Mud

There Are Horses

Invisible World

BLUE MUD

PIANO STOOL

You sit on a piano stool and play
nothing at all, merely stare at the keys
as if they were waiting for another. You stay
facing their silence for hours, your knees

bent softly beneath the lip of the piano.
You hear music your mother played, or your aunt's
soft fingers sliding from key to key with no
idea of what she would hit next. With a glance

you watch the cat climb the stairs, see
a Buick pass the front window. You are in love
with music, with the way it pleads
with you. Suddenly you lift your hands above

the keys and pounce on them. Thick fingers
that cannot find the music, only sounds
that animals make when trapped. Noises that linger
to deafen the room even after the lid is back down.

You walk to the other side
of the room and sit in a hollow of the noise
knowing that they are your notes, but you decide
that you hate them and that boys

with big hands lose the music so easily while
those with delicate hands can shape their own style
from the keys. Sitting for hours on the piano stool
making music, while others practice ridicule.

SILENT ACCUSATIONS

Sometimes I see that a man's body
is difficult to dream with
its muscles tightening too quickly
at a sound or caress.
I stretch out my fingers
and my palm looks innocent
almost vague. Yet with it
I could cover a mouth
or bruise the flesh of a child.

I hold them behind my back
to avoid their silent accusations.

VOICE

Today eight months pregnant, you rise slowly
from the bed. Your mother's death sucks
the red from each rose friends have sent.

Inside you, our new child feels
your pain also but he does not
know what to do with it.

Before you go to bed, you sing to him
and for the first time, I hear
your mother's voice come out of your mouth.

THE MUSIC

"I'm hungry," you say,
and for some reason
I think of your mother
playing piano at Christmas.
Her piano quiet now
rests in our house.
I bring you a plate full of fruit
and as you eat
I hear notes coming from below us,
notes that on their own
would make no song.
I remember us making love
at your mother's house
when we were going to university
and lived with her,
filling her basement with intimate sounds.

I like waking in your arms,
your kisses finding me
sometimes before the birds.
Today, though, it's the music
I am haunted by,
your mother waking us one Christmas morning
before we moved out
and I went upstairs and watched her
alone at the piano.
I saw how little I understand mothers.
I watch you do things
with the children
you learned from your mother.

It is your sister who still
plays the piano, who gets up
early on Christmas to repeat
what her mother once did.

In our new house I am drawn
by the music, but you
ignore it, kissing me instead.

And I am torn between the music
and you, and I want to learn
to play for you and the children
on Christmas morning, to fill
the house with what must have been
there before, long ago.
But I can't ignore your kisses
making me quiver in new places.
I close my eyes and let the music go,
holding you instead.

In one of your drawers you keep
a lock of your mother's hair
from when she was our daughter's age.
But I have never seen you take it out.
Some nights I think of the lock of hair
there near our bed
and I am happy.
I sneak out of the room then
and go to sit at the piano.
Sometimes I even rest my hands
over the keys.
But in the end I return to bed.

I close my eyes
and wait for sleep,
the music inside me but nowhere else.
I imagine that you hear it too,
in your sleep perhaps
or as you pass the piano
or when you caress me,
my eyes saying
something that surprises you.

BLUE MUD

As I lie beside you near daylight
do you hear me dream about my father
and his story of blue mud?
One dry summer all the water
disappeared from the ponds beside the house
and there was nothing
but a blue mud left caking in the sun.
He walked across the mud
and imagined himself
at the bottom of a huge lake
and for the first time
the sky and earth were the same colour.

He lost his teeth one by one
until he could not say
"I love you" clearly.
Mirrors told him he was old
and he did nothing.
His light-coloured pants
were covered in blue dust
and he liked that
would taste it on
his fingertips and smile.
Years later I would take his hand
and ask him about the blue mud
and you would listen
from the living room
your mouth closed
your arms filled
with our new son.

All kinds of creatures
lived in the blue mud
and when their homes
were exposed they burrowed
far into the mud
not too eager for the sun.
Sometimes he would take a shovel
and dig some of them up
and put them into burlap bags
and carry them
back towards the house
where I was sleeping.
I knew him as my father
even though I cannot say
who he is even now.
Through him I remember blue mud.

As I dream of the sun
I think also
of your body next to mine
expecting it to tell me
what it is you want
but it doesn't and can't
just as my body
doesn't own its desire.
As I wake
my body wakes with me
and spills into the room
and I follow after it
uncertain what else to do.

I look at my fingers
and everywhere else
for a sign of blue mud
but there is none.

Coming back from the blue mud
my father would wake me
and show me the things
he had found
and I would watch him stir his tea
and whistle to himself
as if he was taken by a grand idea.
I would stand off at a distance
watching him become
in new ways my father.

My father's god had no hands
nor eyes, nor could he speak.
He was not a man or a woman
nor a lover but something
that climbed into his head
each day and stayed there.
Something that did not speak
to him but moved with him
and he understood the pressure
of moving through a life
with a god he could not remove.
My father's god had no power
it could not teach him
anything or me anything
and most of the time

I could feel my father
taking care of his god
though he did not speak about him
or even mention the word god.
God was always small
and insignificant.
All it was possible to learn
from such a creature
was where the soul began inside.

Eventually we moved away
and my father lost
the blue mud forever.
Now when he speaks of it
he grows sad
and I love him for it.
He plays with my son
and I can see his soul
on his fingertips
as he raises my son
into the air.
He speaks slowly to Austin
as if my son might be his own.
And I can still see
the blue mud on his fingers
as he holds my son
the dust rubbing off
on Austin's face.
And they both laugh.

Finally I see why my father liked
the blue mud so much
because it was something
he could carry back
into the house.
It was something
that could be left
on those he loved
without hurting them
and as he turned back to them
he could see his imprint
left behind
something small and glowing
something that would soon
rub off but was there
at least for awhile
and he must have smiled
as I do now
thinking of my son
as an old man
waiting by a window
for his grandson
the soul not such
a fearful thing after all.

NOTHING VANISHES

1

My mother picks mushrooms
out in the bush, small hands
reaching between the thistles
perfectly, never once getting
nicked. She doesn't worry about
picking poisonous ones.
She knows what they look like
and avoids them.
Her fingers, smelling musty
from all those mushrooms,
reach up from the earth
to touch me.

Mushrooms line the table
and she cuts through some
and washes others and she
offers me one and I look at it
for awhile and then
put it in my mouth,
never sure if it is poisonous or not.
Her fingers have remained young
despite everything.
As she cleans the dirt from
beneath a nail later,
she sings softly to herself.
I want to join in but don't,
just listen as the past lingers
outside every window and all
I can taste is mushrooms for hours after.

2

She boils rice on the wood stove
and fries some of the mushrooms
and tastes one now and then.
She doesn't care what I'm thinking
or what the fire begs her to do.
She ignores everything but her cooking—
the mushrooms pulled quickly, authoritatively
from the stove.

After supper my mother
puts the rest of the mushrooms
in the fridge hiding them
in various brown paper bags.
Tomorrow after I return to the city
she will continue to eat them,
looking at them on her plate,
gentle reassuring shapes.
For a moment they might look
ruined, all shrivelled there
waiting to be consumed,
becoming once more what the earth
expected. And as she eats them,
somewhere inside her she
loses and finds again her God.
Her soul is something she thinks of
as she looks at her young fingers.
Her son so far away calls to ask
about the mushrooms, but doesn't,
asking about something else instead.

3

New mushrooms come up to replace
the ones she picks.
In a few weeks she will go out
to collect them, returning
to familiar rocks and trees.
Sometimes while picking mushrooms
she will kneel to pray,
the bush so quiet her heart
forms a thunder around her.
I can almost hear her prayers
as I imagine her kneeling before
a certain pine tree.
Its not the words I hear
but the murmurs between each word,
long and certain coming from
where I imagine her soul to be.
When she stands again her legs are shaky
and I reach out a hand to steady her
but touch the window of my office
instead. Opening my eyes
the city looks aimless as it
vanishes at the horizon.
The earth beneath her feet
supports her as my outstretched hand can not.

4

I don't buy mushrooms in the supermarket
but walk past them and see my mother
turning her nose up at them,
tame and small on the counter.
She is what I will dissolve into.
I am what she has left the world
and my skin no different than hers
washes in the sunlight and does not
shine but reflects a dull image
of something bright.

5

I do not send her flowers or telegrams
just show up now and then,
expecting to eat mushrooms
and to talk.
When my plate is empty
I will lay down my knife and fork
knowing that when God comes
he can do no damage
or provide any answers,
because the only answers there are
I have already found:
my stomach full, the night
still a few hours off,
and my mother moving about
her small house as if
she were already in heaven.

DEATHNESS

One winter my mother
was lost out in the snow for hours
her tracks disappearing
at the edge of the bush.
My father hurdling through
waist high snow.
My mother made a cave in the snow
and slept there, her fingers
nearly blue when my father found her
and carried her home without
waking her as if trying to
preserve her dreams.

Hours later she woke in her bed
and did not know us,
looked into our eyes
as if we were people
she had found in her sleep.
Father made her tea
and she took it gingerly
as if it contained a fire she feared.
I could see her trying not to
melt as she drank.
Still she did not speak
but rose out of bed and
walked slowly to the door
and then turned back at the last
moment and threw her cup
into the garbage as if that
were the proper thing to do.

The wood stove was hot
and she sat before it for hours

memorizing what the fire told her.
She looked at the pictures on the wall
ones she had hung there
years ago, and she tried to
recognize them but could not.
She asked me about them
as a visitor might.
Once she placed her face
just inches from a photo
of her parents taken when
she was just a girl.
She lifted one finger
to her mouth and then to the glass
and rubbed it trying to remove
a stain or bruise of dust.

Later that night my father
took her to bed with him
and held her as if he wanted
to drain the cold out of her.
She lay still, not speaking
claiming small parts of the room
with her eyes.
She never once touched my father
or called out to him.
I spent most of the night
huddled in front of the wood stove
waking now and then to put in more wood.
In the dark the snow outside
shone through the window
as if it were
looking for us to offer again
its deathness.

Near morning a dog howled across
the lake and I woke
finding myself huddled before
a cold stove. I did not want to
wake my parents by lighting
the fire again, so I went off
to my own bed, its cold covers
wrapped around me like the morning.
As I slept, I dreamed of
mother standing by the front door
in summer holding her dress down
from the wind. I was near her
and could smell her breath and
I wanted to tell her about winter
but she was watching
something on the horizon.
I fixed my eyes on her
and felt the skin on my hands shrink.

When I awoke my mother was standing
over me as if she had been
watching me sleep for hours.
Her bad teeth showed through
her lips as she bent down to kiss me.
At the door to my room my father stood
barely visible behind my mother
and he was smiling too
as if his body could easily claim this room.
I wanted to burrow under the covers
then but I didn't. Instead, I said :
"Mother are you okay?" She did not answer
but with her eyes she showed me
where to look and as I did
I could see the snow was gone.

1

He loved my mother even after she went crazy
and climbed in a stranger's car
headed for Winnipeg or anywhere my father
might not find her.
But he brought her home again
expecting in the morning she would be gone.
But she stayed
and accepted his simple ways
even though she knew
there were demons everywhere
that he couldn't see.

2

He would take me with him to gather wood
and he would sometimes stalk a deer
not to kill it but to watch it
as it wandered through the bush.
His life was not something he needed
to run away from. His place in it changed
all the time but that made it safer.
There was no time to sit back
and think about adventures or to dream
a life your son might wake up happy in.
What was important was knowing where
the sun was in the sky.

3

History branches in a different direction
from him and only a few will notice
how sunlight and love gave him pleasure.
I will remember him holding flowers
on the day I was married kind of shy
but going wild on the dance floor
sweeping past everyone so graceful and true
mastering his life so perfectly
but careful all the same
to leave room for his son.

4

What we leave behind is grown over
faster than most of us imagine.
The world pulls in
so many directions even a god
could not keep the path clear.
What we throw out along
the way is collected by those
who have no interest
in the origins of such things.
The chair my father sits in each day
doesn't wait for him —
it could just as easily conform
to another's shape.

5

I watch him drink a beer
his hands directing his words
as if he was leading up to something.
He tells me how he rode horses
when he was young, how he never used
a stirrup even though nearly everyone else did.
He would wash them down
sad quiet creatures who endured
out of love.
His horse was brown with a white nose
and he called him Charlie.
He loved the smell and feel of the horse
as he rode him down
the thin gravel road to town.
Once in awhile a car
would pass but the horse was never spooked,
just hugged the edge of the road
as my father had taught him.

6

No one remembers Charlie, only my father
sitting with his beer, moving now and then
to avoid the sunlight.
Once he fell from the horse and broke
his hand and he shows me the scar.
He is glad to have something
to show me from his youth.
I can't see the scar no matter how hard
I look. His hand is worn and rough

as I remember, but now I see too that
it is slowly succumbing to arthritis.
In the past it was changed for good
by that single fall,
but only my father knows how
opening and closing it
placing a beer back in its grip
feeling only what he can feel.
His hand made him strong for awhile.

7

When I was a boy I had no idea
history sometimes carries warnings.
I didn't see what was there
when I woke in the morning
was not there when I went
to bed at night.
My father usually was a dark figure
who wandered through my life whether
it was safe or not.
He never examined his love or gave names
to anything that he felt
just let his life flow from him
touching those around him sometimes softly
sometimes hard. In his head he carried history
and memories he had no desire
to tell to anyone including me.
I fought with him, called him bastard,
liar, not waiting to see
the world he wrapped around me
was more of his making

than I thought. Some nights he
would wake me with his drunken wanderings
through the house, making my life
a story for someone to tell
late at night when there is nothing
else to do. He didn't want to be saved
wanted no part of such things.
Unlike my mother and me who
wanted only to be certain that a god
could provide such a service if it was needed.

8

Sometimes when he shaved he whistled
and looked closely in the mirror
looking for something there.
Night was information
we carried over into morning.
I would stand in front of the slop pail
and look into its rancid contents
and wonder how our bodies and life produced
such things. My father never used it
just peed outside even at 40 below
taking his time watching the mist
lift gently from his stream.
He would turn back to me when he was done
doing up his zipper with a smile.
I would cough into my hands or turn away
not exactly afraid, just uncomfortable
with the ease with which he could do such things.
In front of the slop pail I would listen
to the house around me begging

not for anything in particular, just begging.
And my life had too much data to write down.
After peeing I would go back to my room
and read something or listen to the wind outside
waiting, just as I do now,
my father in another room
his life formless and proofless.

9

Only history waits behind us
like the stream from a passing boat.
Those that believe it or read it will never
know my father and how he broke his hand
or rode his horse into town
shrinking carefully into the dark each night
making his way as best he could
not complaining or joining in on anything
but participating just the same.
His healed hand stuffed in a pocket
feels a coin or two or a lighter
nothing important to pull out and show someone.
His hand will stay there fiddling
with something neither perfect nor with blame —
a simple hand that could caress someone or sign
his name — and he looks away knowing what you sign
is not that important after all, will not
make your life any different, can only
please someone with money or power for a little while.
And then, slowly,
bit by bit, the elements
will do the rest.

I undress and you
lie on the bed with
your hands open
giving me something
to taste on your palm.
Your eyes are closed,
the skylight hums with light.
I close my eyes and see you
as still as the living can be.
I begin to dance for you
first my fingers then arms then all
of me and you answer back
move for move and then I answer
you and we sweat together
old and young at the same time
saved by orgasms
from growing cold.
I speak in tongues for you
moving my mouth to where
you call me and alone
like this we claim each
our own pleasure.
Our lovemaking
without opposites
no longer man and woman
using murmurs instead of words.
Signals learned from the beginning
of the world learned
and let out when together
speaking in tongues until
morning fits around us like a new skin.

THERE ARE HORSES

HIDDEN

All is hidden.
Including what bodies are
and how they stand
so gently in a landscape.
Bodies accumulate blame and love
without patience or understanding.
They remain hidden.

There is evil in my hand,
in my arm, in my fingers,
and my head is a world
without accompaniment,
without the shock of shape,
without the waiting.
The world is hidden
and we know its beauty that way.
And my voice hidden
by the sounds it forms.

My body is cold, directionless
as I stand not far from you
and watch as you undress
and our bodies listen to themselves
and know the cries that linger
beneath the surface
waiting not for voice
nor for longing
but for instruction.
You ache as you circle me
and I crave you.

Our bodies are only
capable of murmurs
and moans, wordless
questions pushed into the air
not by mouths or lips
but by the throat.
We are pulled forward
or at least think of it
as being pulled forward
when nothing answers us,
not the light
nor what we breathe in our sleep.
We remain hidden, lying together
letting our bodies move us along
no longer certain
what to touch first.

Our children fasten
themselves to the rooms
where we leave them to sleep.
We speak to them
of love and death
and they pretend we are right.
Each has fallen asleep in our arms
and we have waited
before lowering them into their beds
and we did not think of their souls
or how we are the ones
and not our children
who must learn from their sleep.

For many years I have forgotten
about the soul
and how it remains hidden
not disguised or covered,
just hidden in some place
where it can not be corrupted
nor changed. I think about it
lost inside me somewhere
but that is wrong.
It's not inside me
or even a part of me
but is hidden
some place away from me
watching me
knowing that no matter what I do
it is not affected.
It does not wear me
nor consume me nor instruct me,
merely watches as if
I might be a story
it was learning to tell.
It could not fill my hands
nor could I carry it with me
from a burning building.
So I go back to forgetting it.
Most of the time my soul
is far away, not real,
not known, not captured,
not held, just hidden,
something it is best to forget
while living my life
as if there was no soul at all.

CHURCH BELLS

The morning is filled with a strong wind and a thin smoke from a distant forest fire. At the end of the block a church bell sounds and people from across the city park their cars up and down the street. I stand in the near dark of my house and think of salvation as something easy, something people occupy their time with because it helps them understand the sounds they hear at night. I don't want salvation or anything remotely like it. I want to follow that smoke filming over my windows. I want to follow it to a fire that doesn't burn but sings as if an angel was caught in it somewhere.

It's those people I think of parking their cars neatly. Some of them carry their children in their arms others walk with them hand in hand. I see that they are gentle people who have ended up in their lives by accident and that it doesn't matter anyway because somewhere inside they are continuing to count things. Their children move through the smoke as if it were coming from the breath of God on a cool day. I hear them sing as they walk or skip, even though their mouths never open. Their world thuds against mine and as I drink a glass of water I think about the god they see each night before them, their parents sitting in another room reading a book or just listening. I know that somewhere behind me or upstairs my own children are playing and I hear nothing as if their lives leave no trace except to themselves. I imagine them walking through walls to get to me, to stand beside me and whisper: "I love you" — just as I do every night when I put them to bed. They do not feel the floor shake or know the news that spills out of the TV. Even if I let days pass without turning it on, the News waits inside it for me, building to something hideous. It's not that I want to protect them from my life or a world I have not told them about, but like those parents going to the church I want a miracle to be there when they finally cross over into this dark room where I am standing.

After a while the church is full, and I go to my door and open it. Standing at the door half in darkness and half in light, I feel what God might feel apprehending this world we lift up to him or her for praise. I see too that going to church is a way of talking to ourselves out loud. A way to let the voices out that have built up over the years. But what do those children think as they stand or sit beside their parents and hear those strange voices coming out of their own mouths.

Someday I want to cross the street and enter into the church, standing at the back while the minister speaks or the congregation rises to sing a hymn. Not because I want to understand them or to join them or to hear exactly what it is they want to do with their lives. There are many other ways to worship than this. No, I want to go to the church because it is on my street and sometime my children might look at it and ask me what goes on in there and I want to be able to take them inside to hear the new voices coming from within them.

They have already started to look into books of their own, have already started to catch a glimpse of the News from over my shoulder. Each day the house they live in gets a little weaker. Soon it will no longer be the house they were born to but some place to escape. The world will be what calls them and they will answer its call walking out into the street into the smoke and wind not looking back but ahead forming their own lines, standing in their own windows, feeling the earth open in random places for them. And passing that church they may enter or they may not. It won't matter what I have said or believed. All that will matter for them is that one night alone each of them will have heard a new voice inside them and each will have decided on their own how best to let it out.

BLUE HORSE

Our two-year old son likes to look at pictures of animals
and to say their names.
In his room after I put him to bed,
I hear him saying those names like a chant,
sleep coming slowly.
As I drop him off at the day care,
he likes to touch the picture of the horse
they have hung up on the wall.
He giggles and buries his face in my shoulder.
He doesn't know about the sadness of animals yet,
the ones taken each day from the world.
I am uneasy when I hear him saying their names,
practising already to remember them
in extinction.

He calls our two cats by the same name.
He hasn't learned yet that
it is hard to speak to animals,
that even these cats tolerate us
but don't admire us.
He likes to colour pictures of animals.
He always uses the yellow crayon
so his books are filled with yellow elephants and zebras.
It is sad how we lose the love for animals
letting them save us without doing anything in return.

Our son's favourite story is Goldilocks.
He likes to see the bears waking her
to watch as she flees frightened out of the house.
I am not sure what the story is teaching him,
but I read it each time he asks for it.
He is more fascinated by the bears than Goldilocks,
taking particular delight in seeing the inside of their house.

Someday he will learn that bears' houses
don't look at all like the one in the story.
Such a house would make them unhappy
with its large mortgage.
But perhaps the baby bear does feel the awful responsibility
of being the baby,
and perhaps the momma bear really is the middle sized one,
and perhaps the papa bear is proud of his loud voice.
I don't like the stereotypes
and try to read the story changing the roles,
but Austin makes me go back
to what it was.

He learns too much from animals,
takes as truth what their stories are.
Perhaps he will one day go swimming and look for mermaids.
And I want him to be gentle,
to learn it is a caress that holds power,
not a slap.
I want him to keep saying the names of animals
before going to sleep.
I want him to know the grace these animals have,
and to hear what an animal in distress sounds like.

Sometimes before going to sleep
he will make the sound of a lion or dog.
And I wonder if he is searching inside
for a sound of his own.
Will he let me hear it or will he take it away with him
when he moves out,
hiding it until he is far enough away?
I want to ask him what a father should do
to keep love in the room.

Tonight as I put him to bed
he brings out a book of zoo animals
and we name them together.
He watches my mouth as if some part of my soul clung there.
He repeats the names after me, smiling and laughing.
For a short time he reaches out to touch each page,
to feel what might linger in that flat kingdom.
In one book a blue horse blends partly into the horizon.
He likes that blue horse
and lingers on that page for some time,
stroking the horse's mane.
He takes my hand and places it on the horse's mane too.
He talks to the horse after I have left him for the night.
As I listen I think of the animals
that take on the stories we make up for them.
The blue horse waits to finish his jump,
caught forever as part of the sky.

THERE ARE HORSES

In the morning down the street
there are horses waking. Casually
they turn to one another, nodding their heads
nearly in meter. Each horse floats in flesh
formed on moist nights in the foothills.
The mountains require bravery and
a knowledge of how poetry enters one's head
at night shapeless and beautiful
clothed in a dull murmur. In the foothills the horses
run alone, hooves lifted high above the grass.
No one comes to the fields to watch the horses.
Traffic passes a few miles away as though
in another century. None of those passing
feel any pity for these creatures
darting near the horizon. If you asked
people in the cars on the highway,
they would describe God exactly like one of the dark
horses in the distance. Except they would
not say that, trying too hard
to mean something else.
Each would look away when speaking of God
as though he might be seen out of the corner
of the eye. The horses would approach it differently.
Perhaps first taking a run across
a small field and then jumping
the fence, they would be gone
down several pastures before we would have
formulated the next question.

We don't listen well when other creatures speak.
The slow howl of a wounded animal makes us
feel uncertain, alone. When re-entering the city

have formed when they were alone and could no
longer speak to anyone. We hear the horses behind
us even though they stopped running hours ago.
In the rear view mirror we see nothing except
perhaps a bit of dust lifting from the shoulder
of the road. Perhaps we pull over then and try
to catch our breath while the motor idles.
The horses were never ours, just visitors for awhile.
But like them we ignore our private shame for the good
of others, ignore the steam of our breath on a cold
fall morning. Instead we know that the horses are
nearly all gone now, only a few of them spotted
occasionally at the side of the road. Sometimes we
think we would prefer to encounter whole packs
of them, noble and brave as they waited for their
first rider. As condemned creatures they seem
to not carry their weight as well, backs swayed.
Other horses, not these wild ones, inherit a little
less each generation, content to wait in shopping malls
while small children pay two dollars for a ride.
But these wild ones still bear a skeleton in common
with the other horses. The gods do not tame creatures
but leave them wild because only wild creatures
serve a god best. Not gods ourselves, we haven't
learned this yet. Instead, we form creatures carelessly
in our own image. At night south of this city, wild horses
sleep in coulees listening all night for the breath
of a wolf near an ear. They are at home anywhere
and do not need to be told when to rest.
It is their eyes we cannot face and the violence there
that they never let die. Half crazed ourselves,
we roam through fields — and now and then
lift a rifle and fire.

ENEMY

"Why do we have enemies?" my daughter asks and I want to
say that we don't, but she already knows about the war in the
Gulf. When she was younger I might have lied to her like I did
at first about the death of her grandmother, but now I can't and
she waits at the dinner table for some truth. Whatever I offer
her will sound wrong or sad and perhaps she will run into
another room wanting to be alone. I'd like to tell her that I
have no enemies and that she doesn't either, but that is not what
she wants to hear or believe. Sometimes I am her enemy as I
stand outside her door waiting for her to open it and let me enter
once more into her life. I suppose whatever I tell her now she
will forget. It still matters to me how I will answer. I would
like to pick her up and hold her and not have to say anything,
but that won't do. Finally I say it is because an enemy defines
who we are and what matters to us. I can tell that either she is
disappointed or does not believe me and I don't want to go on
with my life without finding an answer we can both live with.
But I would feel foolish phoning my parents and asking them
such a thing, yet I don't know who else to call. I think about all
the books scattered about my office. There is not a single one I
could pick up and read what she wants to hear. So I stand in
my house in this comfortable city and wait for a voice, for any
help I can get even if later I will denounce it.

I think about the daily bombings in the Gulf and the TV singing
praises for our side while the enemy is always kept in the dis-
tance. I hear a girl in Baghdad asking her father about the
bombs that come every night and all he can do is tell her to pray
as they pass another night huddled in a bomb shelter. In war,
even a foolish, sad war like this one, everyone lies. The living,
the dead, the gods — all lie. Bravery has more to do with
killing than with saving lives. During war the gods hide and
those of us who look to them for guidance feel suddenly alone,

everything we do is wrong. Those at home are in the audience
and even the generals call it "In Theatre" as if what was most
important was putting on a good show. The gods don't watch
because they know better and stay hidden, closing their eyes and
ears until they know it's safe.

My daughter forgets the war most days. She still has the luxury
to do so. It is easy to forget it here simply turn the TV to a
rerun of some kind, or open a book you have wanted to read for
a long time. War is fiction shaped more by the dreams of those
who mimic it or carry its vulgar values in their heads. Each war
is carefully slotted into its place in history as if what is import-
ant is getting the order of wars right.

When I tuck my daughter in tonight I try to answer her question
again. I tell her that there should be no enemies, but there are
because sometimes we run out of love and close our eyes and
attack. Some of us can't help being someone else's enemy.
Most of the time we aren't ever really sure why we do what we
do. After the destruction stops and all is quiet, we look around
and begin to see it wasn't our enemies that we were attacking.

I'm afraid that she will wake in the night and listen for bombers,
even though I have told her that the war is far away. Tonight
she grinds her teeth and I hear her as I pass her room. Each life
starts in a simple ordinary way, but somewhere along the way
terror seeps in a little at a time. She and I are safe for now, yet
as long as there is war somewhere, one of us will wake during
the night to listen, and night by night we will lose a bit more
sleep.

MOVING THROUGH THE LIGHT

My son holds a doll
and feels comfortable
does not know yet
that there is danger
or that this house he explores
is not what his father means by love
or how his father
would like to show him love
but I am used to the simple disguise of things
and my life is proven to me
not by myself
but by those I love
those who don't want the kind of wisdom
I am trying to form inside.
I have no wisdom, no learned things
only a small knowledge
of what to abandon
and what to hold onto.

We are whole, our bodies
moving through the light
not to find darkness or a stronger light
but to find out what bodies and light are.
Our bodies sustain damage
are healed for awhile
but learn new ways to fail, to grow old
and we run not into the streets
but inside our minds
run from thought to thought
not worrying what should be connected
or what it might mean
or if a god could stitch it all for us.

My son sings while he waits for supper
and I am a shadow across his face
and I can name this knowledge I let
pass through me to him
but he doesn't care
looks instead not at me or what
I am about to say
but at something he sees in the other room
something he will never tell me
and love has no beginning place
in a room and yet it is felt everywhere
and my son holds up a bird and kisses it
and I know that what passes between us
is not wisdom but love and it explains
not what should be done but what things
feel like and that's okay
because I am his father for only a little while
and I don't want to take that for granted.
I want him to see that when I am not
in this room
I might be the sentence
he is about to utter.
He hands me the bird and I kiss it too
and release it out the window
and it is not the sky it seeks
but a freedom from our kisses.
There is nothing we can do to hold it back.
The wind helps carry it to where we are nothing
but another building below it somewhere.

FIRE ACROSS THE STREET

There was a fire across the street
last night and I heard a child call
its mother. This morning when I awoke
in bright light I could hear the child
calling still. I went out to the front porch
but the house was standing,
no fire, nothing but the black snow of December.

The chinook has uncovered a toy
Breanne left on the front yard.
You and she are at your mother's
and I listen as the traffic charges
down a side street. Objects are true
the false is in the words we use
to name the true. Sometimes the house
across the street is gutted and sometimes
it is not. Truth might be sensual
or incomplete, or it might be
the obsession of the least godlike.
False things depend on a god's knowledge.

While I sleep the fire returns
the house has no will and cannot be false.
The fire burns because of the truth of fire.
Even when it rains or snows the fire continues
to burn and sometimes I watch and listen as
the child calls but I do nothing. I do not
try to find the child or the mother.
I know if I did I would find
no one, for the fire is my way of believing —
it belongs to my true nature.

I cannot say what effect truth has on
my life or the way I love you and listen
as you move around downstairs full
of purpose, proud of your feelings.
I accept certain things as true because
they have a likeness I admire. I expect that
equation is universal. I think
my work has a purpose and virtue
that is neither divine nor evil.
Still each morning I awake expecting a fire
across the street and there is none.

Across the street in a park three girls are hiding from one
another as the melting snow fades their footprints. You watch
as their breath nearly reaches your cheek. From this distance
they would be easy to find, but they remain hidden from each
other awaiting discovery. It occurs to you to cross the street to
whisper in their ears where the others are hiding. Instead,
something calls you away from the window and you feel as
though part of you remains waiting for the girls to disappear,
their game no longer appealing to them.

The light inside the house is dull and you stumble forward
expecting to fall over an edge, to trip forward onto metal. At
the door of the baby's room, you are hidden by the absence of
windows. You enter and find her sitting in her crib trying to
stand. Your back is still warm from the sunlight.

This morning your mother called to report on the breakup of
your brother's marriage and you listened as though trying to
catch the breathing of someone else on the line. When you put
down the phone it seemed your life was getting darker each day.
You remembered the words that your brother spoke at sixteen,
looking across the room at a group of girls, picking out his bride
from the look on her face. You listened then as you did today,
not sure how to accept another's life revealed to you.

Today all you can think about is light, and how it changes what
we feel, how we wake in it and sleep when it's gone. Your
daughter's hiccups bring you again to her crib, still not sure if
you can get her to take her nap or not. Even in her short life
the light is there shaping her knowledge, her growth in this
small but comfortable room. Last night the moon stayed in one
window all night and when you woke it was still there daring
you to make it move. But you ignored it, looked instead at the

sunrise, lifted your hands above your head as though
surrendering.

It's been weeks since you felt your body explode as it ignored
the light in another's eyes. Now at the top of the stairs near
your daughter's room, you cough quietly, trying not to wake her.
Standing there you know there are things missing, that it's
impossible to complete your life while you are still standing and
waiting for the hours to descend. As long as you can look out a
window there is hope, as long as you can defy the light there is
hope. If God was merely a ticking bomb you expected to go
off, perhaps things would be simpler, you could understand the
delay better. Instead, this first day of spring with the snow
outside, you have learned to listen exactly, to see where the fire
stops at the doorstep. You watch as a dog sniffs at the snow.

You go back to the window to see again the young girls playing
in the park. But they have gone, if they were ever there at all.
The park is empty. Even now as you watch, it is losing its
cover of snow. Beneath, a brown layer of earth emerges,
looking vulnerable and worn.

I EXPECT THE DEVIL

1

I expect the devil to come carrying in his mouth the first words
of my death. I expect him to be old and very male his fingers
as sharp as a butcher's knife. I expect there to be a stink around
him and a ring of darkness no eye can penetrate. I expect him
to ask me to love him, to reach out and offer me everything I
desire. I expect to feel cold, to move my hand and start a fire.
I expect him to offer me a drink of my own blood and for me to
accept it.

I don't expect this ordinary hotel in the middle of Calgary where
children laugh outside as if they are no longer the believers in
any god. Nor do I expect his hands to look beautiful and
young, or his voice to soothe every pain. I don't expect to feel
this love and joy that makes my body heal its cancers. I see so
clearly what before I tried to ignore. I see the souls of all the
riders on a passing C-Train. I see the faces of my own children
as a god will not let me see. There is love even on the faces of
the dead. I open my eyes and he stands back from me and
smiles, offering me nothing, but he waits for me to say
something. I can't. I no longer know words. I sit down on the
floor and put my head between my knees and start to cry. That
is how they find me crying near an open elevator. In it stands a
boy with a strange perfume. They do not look inside the
elevator but lift me to the waiting ambulance, its window
shielding me from onlookers.

2

A god can't be looked at. She comes as I expect her to, when I
sleep. Her mouth opens my dream and her lips are a sweet fruit
I test with my tongue. I live in this dream for so many nights,

when I wake I will need a debriefing. She draws rooms in my dream and I follow her from room to room and feel her fury as it vanishes over our heads like a gust of wind. Behind us somewhere there are singers and guitar players. When I swallow I taste wine and I expect she will make love to me and I will want her to leave her fury on me like a scent I can carry after. I will close my eyes then and wake up knowing every smell is her. I will crave her and that will be wrong. I will take an elevator in a fire, an elevator that opens on my floor as if sent for.

But when I meet her she is old, nearly blind, as she moves awkwardly about my house. I don't know whether to call her lover or mother and instead I say nothing. She smashes some pottery as she knocks over a table. She wants to see the children and like a grandmother takes candy out of her pockets. She talks about heaven as though it was a summer cottage she grows tired of. Her bones make a tender music as she walks. She sways more than walks, and I would have called it beautiful if I still had such a vocabulary. In her pockets she carries the souls of many. They are small like bath beads brightly coloured and she holds them in her hands so gently. But they leave their colours on her palms. I know she has no body, no father, no husband, and yet she speaks of each as if she wanted me to know what her life was like. I want to tell her to stay, to live here, to learn how I love my children, my life, to see how my heart delights at what she has dragged through my open door. Still I do not speak but imagine that she can read my thoughts, but she doesn't, has no time for what my life might teach her. For a while, I am someone to entertain, to help move peacefully to a darkness she cares little to enter. When I do speak, she is gone. The first words from my mouth come too late to reach her.

My daughter says: "I can't believe there ever was nothing." This implies: "I can't believe there ever will be nothing." I want to hold her but tell her instead: "I can't believe either." As if my company is what she wanted.

Infinity: what Rebecca's mouth means when she wakes me with kisses so late at night the clocks have gone quiet. Or my mother watching my plane take off from the Winnipeg airport as she wears the pink sweat suit I gave her last year for Christmas. Or all the pictures in the hall, each one filled with people who feel they belong somewhere else.

Infinity: a poet photographed, sitting with her arms folded, and her smile asking you to visit sometime.

Infinity is the day a friend phones to say his brother just died in a car accident, his voice sounding like the day a gang of boys beat him up in grade five. At the other end of the line my friend describes his brother's accident, how he walked around after thinking he only had a broken leg and then hours later he was in a coma. His own daughter asking later what a coma is, as if the hurt could be taken away.

Infinity is knowing that out beyond the moon and sun, galaxies wait as if they too wanted to tell a story.

Most of the time I try to forget it. Skip over the word in books, interested more in small things like a kiss. But now I see that infinity is knowing there will always be something new. As bodies clamber for air and light, something passes from them that can't be retained.

Infinity starts to grow inside us somewhere and all we can do is watch.

CHANCES

Chances are that we will
grow weary in the evening's chill.
Holding hands we can warm
each other while infinity

looms in each direction.
Our noses find the scent
the gods left us to follow.
Lying in the grass

we let the stars
hypnotize us.
And we hold fast

until we are sure
we won't clutter the sky
with our flight

INVISIBLE WORLD

WAITING IN THE DARK

I remember getting off the school bus
on a cold night in February not wanting
to look up the road, afraid the lights
might not be on and the dark empty house
invisible at the end of the road.
Later I made the fire in the wood stove
as my younger brother collected wood.
Dad was in town somewhere drinking, forgetting about
supper and the two boys who waited alone ten miles
in the bush. Their mother 300 miles away
in a mental hospital. I waited with my brother
in front of a grey TV screen watching
Ben Casey and the crazy way it began: *Man, Woman, Infinity.*
The word *Infinity* sounded as cold as
the face of the window behind my neck. The faint glow
of the dangling light bulb was the only finite thing left.
I could not go to the window could not look out
into the snow to watch for the headlights of Dad's truck.
As I remember now, I think not of the cold or the waiting
but of the darkness broken occasionally
by the flash of headlights on the Trans Canada.
I think of being just nine years old
and learning that the darkness stays inside and lingers
even on the nights when I found the lights on,
Dad waiting, eyes sore from crying
or being alone too long in front of the TV.
Unemployed, he watched the days pass as though
he was shut out forever. He didn't know how a lover's hand
passes in a dream like a kiss or a threat. His wife
300 hundred miles away. He gave up fighting
long ago waiting for me to come home,
an uncomfortable father no longer sure
what the right thing is or what is

noble or good. He had no one to blame.
Even God was a fake
who concealed himself with a beard
or mumbled to those who hid behind
the closed door of a church.
Dad would wait for me to make supper.
I would open cans and toss their contents
into boiling water, turning away to find a window,
any window.

Some winter nights now when I am the first one home,
I enter the empty house expecting to find
my father standing in the dark
whispering to me.
In the corner my mother stands
smiling as though dreaming someone's caress.
I can't forget, can't stop running around
the house turning on lights, pulling down blinds.
Those dark arrivals all those years ago taught me
how we are slowly broken, our parents
just as out of control as we are. Their faces
accepting gestures or expressions that the nerves
created on their own. Impulsively they smile as a child
walks towards them for the first time.
Our minds are sometimes like jelly that bounces around
in our skulls gently bending to fit
the bone structure that contains them.
Each of us stands in a dark doorway
but only those around us see the doorway
or the darkness behind us.
Still I, like others, listen to more stories
as though waiting for an explanation or solution

that will hold me together as I stand
in front of a dark house alone. Inside it
my whole life is pinned to the walls waiting
in its own darkness, in the cold infinity
that surrounds it all the time I am away.

THE WIND INSIDE

1

On board an airplane a boy drops
a glass of water and his mother
smacks his cheek. Those passengers
around her pretend not to notice
but they will remember
the boy did not cry,
only waited for another
blow or a kiss.
He wasn't sure which.
The wind that the plane fought in the sky
was inside him too.
He could feel it sucking him in
until he could say his mother's name
with his whole body.

2

A small girl is chased
by a dog with three legs
and she calls his name over and over
and giggles and she thinks about
her father walking the bottom
of the lake near the edge of the park.
The dog knocks her down
and licks her face. She likes that
and is not afraid of animals.
In the girl's eyes the dog
can see the sky and behind it
a face he should know but doesn't.

The girl's father learned to hold
his breath underwater for a long time
and stays under now for good,
sending news when he can.
Today the girl and dog get up again
to face the wind coming in across the water
and it carries not her father's voice
but a sound from deep in the future,
a sound neither can hear for now.

3

Dressed as an angel, a boy
rides a bicycle. His mother's stern face
is something he feels tattooed onto his back.
On the bicycle he has a soul
and it moves with him and can't be stolen.
He doesn't feel like an angel
nor does he wish
his bicycle could fly.
Behind him his papier-maché wings
flutter in the wind, generated by
his forward motion. He holds
the handle bars so tightly
that he can feel his hands
going numb but he can't let up
or even look back frightened
that something might catch him,
something that will take his wings away
for good. As he pedals, his white shoes
begin to get stained by the oil
from the bike's chain. He doesn't want to stop

and clean them, though. The faster he goes
the stronger the wind feels on his face
and he begins to suck it in. His open mouth
lets it grow in his lungs,
in his stomach, in his heart.
Even that will not make him stop.
He pedals faster and faster
suddenly releasing both hands
from the handle bars
as he moves smoothly into the air.

APPLES

Apples fall to the ground and the boy fills a sack with them and drags it to where his father stands smiling as if life held only mysteries like this. Someday the boy may be a soldier and may die a great distance from this apple tree. The man will already be dead and will never know how his son falls. Now each takes a bite from a different apple and watches the other chewing as if an apple's sweetness could be seen in another's face.

The boy would rather be playing with his friends or in his room, but he likes to feel the apple's flesh swell in his mouth. When he is a soldier, he will think about this day many times, remembering the shape of the apple as it filled his hand. Even when he hoists his gun in the heat of battle and squeezes the trigger, he will imagine that he is holding an apple. But when he dies he will be thinking of something different as the apple in his throat swells until no more air can get around it.

The boy took the sack of apples in to his mother. She will can some of the apples and make pies with others. Later in the kitchen, the boy watched his father wash his hands and turn with them, still damp, to his wife, to kiss her cheek. The boy put one of his fingers in his mouth and it tasted of dirt and apples. As he stood there sucking his finger, his throat began to lose its dryness and his life continued around him and he felt like an apple on a giant tree waiting to ripen. His father passed him, carrying the empty sack back to the yard. The father stood below the empty tree asking himself something that the boy would never hear.

WE GET YOUNGER

We get younger
and do not ask questions
believe the contrary
and let the sun explain
what it can each day.

There is a bird's nest
in the porch
and once a baby sparrow
fell to the floor.
Our cat dragged it
into the house
to teach it
how to live again.

Words don't mean a hell of a lot
when you are sick or dying
and all you can do is
cough up blood now and then
and smile at the nurse
as if she might save you
or something.
Your son opens his mouth
with darkness and does not
speak but looks into your eyes
as if he were trying to find you.

Your body has preferences
but you do not know them
falling asleep in an old chair.
And the city moans away outside
as if in pain.

There is this angel's veil
you brush with your tongue
and you know that love
is the sweet taste of something small
inconsequential
the careful unwrapping of a temptation.

Your stomach produces bile
and most of the time
you are indifferent to that
until it begins
to appear in your mouth
and on your tongue.
You get younger and do not notice
the shape of your backbone
in the mirror.
Your children listen at the door
of your office not yet prepared
for a younger father.
You emerge and they each hug
your leg as if you might
try to escape from them.
You bend down to kiss each one
hoping they might learn something from you
other than the smell of love
as it passes quickly
through a child's life and is gone.
They can feel your aches and pains
can see in your eyes
what you hold back.

They are not afraid even though you are
and they are prepared for everything
because that is what they expect.
You lift up first one and
then the other and close your eyes
and listen to them breathe or speak
and they each get older as you hold them.
And you do not wonder or care
moving your hand across their foreheads
trying to feel their thoughts
trapped behind.

Your son takes what the cat
has left of the young bird
and tosses it out into the yard.
You have to stop yourself
from going after the remains.
Nothing is completed or found
in this house.
You are not afraid to love
nor to explain to your children:
each room could destroy them.

As a young man now you play
with your son in the back yard
and you learn from him the way
each game must be conducted.
Your organs do not give in
neither does your brain
nor your son's imagination.

As the day darkens and the moon
makes an appearance you are both
captured by it and are surprised
you can be changed by something
so distant from your lives.

You think of flesh
not as an escape from darkness
not as something that lures us
into an unbelievable world.
Nor as something lovers cling to
while the world outside
begins to possess them.

You polish the wine glasses
while your wife and children
inhabit other parts of the house.
Each glass looks so meaningless
in your hand as you try to remove
water spots. It would be easy
to drop each one to the floor
until they formed a pile of broken glass.
You move one to your mouth and sniff
for some hint of wine
but all you can detect is
the lingering odour of detergent.
You carefully replace that glass
and lift another and sniff it
as well. Doing this over and over
until all eight are lined one beside
the other on the counter.

You select one at random
and lift it towards the light.
Not a spot left. The glass begins
to tremble in your hand
and you can see all the lines
that cover the skin on your hand
and you return the glass to the others
go out into the living room, the dishtowel
dangling on your shoulder, and you
kiss your wife on the cheek
and you stand beside her for a moment
until the trembling stops
then you go upstairs to collect the children
who by now have aged even more
than you care to see.

AS I GET UP FROM BED

As I get up from bed
you stir and go back
to sleep and I envy you
your quiet slumber
and how it protects you.
I grow tired of being
a man and how I must
fight myself to stay balanced
and most mornings I sneak
downstairs hearing behind me
the sounds my absence makes
and I don't know whether
to smile or cry.

LOVE SUITE
for Rebecca

1

I borrowed your eyes last night
and I walked through
the house wearing them.
Fresh air entered
my lungs and my hands began
to learn tenderness.
Colours were strange,
not at all what I
was prepared for.

You rose from the couch.
I saw my eyes
looking back at me
cold and unsure.

We climbed the stairs together
and went to bed separately.
In the morning, it was
my own eyes I looked out from
and I was afraid.
I saw the colours and sights
that I had once loved
belonged only to my eyes.
I stared out a window and knew
close as we are,
only with our own eyes
can we see our deaths
waiting,
small landmarks on the horizon.

2

I take care to linger
on the places you
have told me to.
You close your eyes
and I like that.
I know your face
and yet each time
it is completely new to me.

You watch me undress.
You say nothing
listening perhaps
to the wind outside.
When I stand naked
you smile and take my hand.
I smile too, my fingers
already finding power.

Everything surprises me:
the way you use your mouth,
the way moonlight finds our bodies
no matter where we lie on the bed,
the way the trees
beyond the window
seem to watch us,
our eyes following
the other's even when
they are closed.
And the way your fingers
seem to be where I want
them to be, the children

not calling out until
our lovemaking is finished
and we lie together
thinking of them
each alone in their small rooms.

And the way you get out of bed
and stand above me as if
you wanted to see how
I appear when alone.

3

I enter the kitchen.
You have placed a rose
in a cup near the sink.
I love the way
its scent covers everything
I touch for the rest of the day.

When I think of you
I do not think of flowers,
the smell of morning
after a night of light rain,
a sweet cloud of perfume
that passes my office.
When I think of you
I do not think of
the full blue dress

that hangs on the door
for the morning
nor the curves
your blue jeans outline.

When I think of you
I do not think
of the warm body
I hug when I wake in the middle
of the night, nor the bathwater
that holds you softly as I
would like to.

All those images remind me
you are unlike the person
I think you are.
You take my hand
when I am tired, when I can
no longer think straight.
You move your hair from your face
and I see there what my eyes keep hidden.

4

Sometimes after making love with you
I look at the moon, how small
we are beneath its scrutiny.

For you I try to be the horizon
or a sound the world makes in spring.
I know I am impatient
and can't place my hands correctly.

I like it when I carry
your scent to work
and sit in my office,
you there with me
lifting me gently to you.

For the rest of the day
I can do nothing but wait
for you to find me
hidden for you.

5

Sometimes I like to wake you
in the middle of the night
and surprise you with my passion.
Our lovemaking is different then
no longer protected by light.
I soothe you awake slowly
my fingers finding you soft and open.
You move your thighs
in a fluid sway as you continue
to sleep. I wash you with my tongue
until you move your hands over me
to tell me you are awake.

When I wake, you are
a field of blossoms beside me.
I take your hand
let it shape my words for me,
your tongue pushing back
the darkness in my mouth.
I hum softly to you.
You smile and I know
how I must open to you,
not be that other man
who sings to himself
while the children cry downstairs,
who finds his pleasure first
while looking into your eyes,
who has not yet learned
his pleasure is formed
by you, his smile
an echo of yours, his words
planted in his mouth by your kiss.

SKIN

We play each other as though
skin is a magic conductor of thought,
the world transfused through lovers,
their embrace allowing history to flow through.
The world changes in sequence, we believe
what we see, accepting the aroma of death.
With crossed eyes we untangle the mess,
wash in dirty water. Lovers as vulnerable as order.
Lovers accepting the wings of paralysed birds.
Our maps torn to pieces, our purposes
written in the eyes of the dying.

INVISIBLE WORLD

You play monopoly with the children
and I fold the clothes
you just finished washing.
I feel this house advertise us.
The invisible world
is where we live most of the time.

A photograph of my father sitting
in the mouth of a cave
makes me think of kissing him
to sense how it feels to grow old.
My mother's grey hair
blows across her forehead as she smiles
and makes me close my eyes.

A bird flew in the front door
and we spent the afternoon trying
to coax it out again.
Once cornered it hovered near
the ceiling as if trying to break through.
When we finally chased it
through the front door,
it circled around
as if coming back and then
veered off into the sky.

My daughter is playing in the next room
with a friend and they pretend
that the world is real.
I listen and I hear myself in her words.
I hear back what I have told her
and it frightens me.

She plays with joy and hope,
her friend laughs too, and both of them
move through the house
as if it were really there,
as if the world were not invisible.
They have both found out already
there is only this house,
this friendship, this love
that can save them, that can
make their lives move smoothly
towards their ends.
As they play, Breanne's room gets bigger
and bigger until it swallows me too.
I continue to type, pretending
I don't hear them.

When I hold you
and think about the invisible world
suddenly I don't care anymore.
I walk over to where my son is playing
and pick him up.
Looking into his one-year-old eyes
I wonder if he is still
trying to become invisible himself.
He pats my face several times and smiles.
Perhaps being invisible is just like this.
The smallest point of light turns
on itself rotating around and around
until it too becomes visible
held for awhile in someone's gaze.

Morning can make us visible too,
just like that, the light
falling onto our bed,
my hand in your hair,
the world outside
pretending to be something else,
as I softly blow into your ear.

TOMATOES

You sent me out for tomatoes
and at a stoplight
I picked one from the bag.
I wanted to bite into it
but didn't, thinking
of your hand running
down my back, your tongue
moving between my legs.
It was at sunset and the sky
listened to my breathing,
a few pink clouds
soothing on the horizon.

At the door you didn't take
the tomatoes but
my lips instead,
covering them with your own,
your tongue filling
every place in my mouth.
We followed the remaining light upstairs.
Our footsteps were
without echoes.

I have learned how to slow
my fingers down, how
your breathing carries guidance.
Over me you were slow and
certain, filling me
with a gracefulness
old bones master reluctantly.

The room, the city, the world
didn't hear us as
your hands followed my thoughts.
Your body led my hands
as they lifted
your thighs toward my mouth.
I sang into you
uttering something from the back
of my throat.
We didn't stop, just slowed down.
My hands washed you
with your sweat.

In the morning I open a window
taking a fresh breath
of cold winter air
cooling what still smoulders.

I find the bag of tomatoes
at the front door, hidden
partially by the morning shadows,
sitting so quiet like a promise.
I leave them there and wait
for you to discover them,
to lift one to your mouth,
your fingers slowly
covered with juice.

FOOLS ON SATURDAY

We are fools on Saturday trying to sleep off a hangover from
the week. The cat watches us as if she were learning the way
humans die. I dream of a landscape covered in hills and it is
snowing everywhere except where I am standing. I feel cold
and listen as wolves follow my tracks while the hills never stop
and I hear someone singing, my mother perhaps or a vagabond
passing over the next hill. All around me are the carcasses of
cows, cold stiff legs pointed like sticks into the sky. I feel as
though I were waking from the dead in the middle of a snow
storm, my teeth chattering, my eyes freezing shut as I walk.
The wind finds my face even though it is pressed into my parka.
I begin to walk perhaps out across a small lake. Trees along the
shore line cracking from the cold. And I say "breathe,"
"breathe" and think of that distant place where your mouth will
open slowly like a rose over my warm flesh. And I hear my
father laughing into a camera, not sure how to pose without
being trapped inside it. I imagine my mother bouncing across
the floor as she walks no longer shy but looking shy from a
distance. We play with our lives as remembered moments hiss
past us in one final extended breath. Still the cold holds me,
rips at my face as I walk and then I think of you. As you speak
your words numb me, make me turn my back against the wind
to stand up straight as I walk and I hear everything in my life
form a chorus to calm the wind and warm the snow beneath my
feet. Slowly I climb from the cold, from the snow, from the
hills and the wolves toward this warm bed, the radio pretending
it's Saturday. The music surrounds me and I sit up in bed,
your face smiling at me from the covers, each of us knowing
how it is to wake so close to our future, so close to our past.

During the night a window breaks and for hours I can't decide if it's the wind or a prowler and I wait to see what morning brings with it. When I rise, I find the living room floor covered in glass as the cool spring air seeps into the room as if looking for me. I go to the front door and throw it open to let in as much of the spring morning as I can. I am safe here protected against the things I have invented or forgotten, clinging to these rooms as if they could prevent death. But the broken glass across the rug shows how far I have drifted.

It is difficult to know the colour God might take in this room. I am safe here but this morning that does not seem good enough even though I will fix the window and then sit out front with my children as if there were no such thing as violence or privilege. Some day my daughter will smoke cigarettes or hang around with strange boys and I will still be waiting on the step for her to come home smiling as she does now acting as if love counted more than anything.

I can take my children to the houses where I grew up on streets where windows were left broken the cold air kept out with old rags. In those places my father would drink until he remembered what he wanted to say and then he would take all night to say the first sentence.

I loved the sounds he made with his mouth as he drank his beer. He would toss an empty bottle at me and I would catch it and he would smile lifting in his hand another full bottle. I wasn't sure what a son does. Most of the time I tried to keep out of the way not hiding just waiting for the right time to leave my bedroom for good.

This morning I pick up the glass piece by piece careful not to cut or nick my skin. As I work I think about the importance of glass. My daughter comes to help but I tell her just to watch afraid she might cut herself. After the glass is all put away I replace the broken pane with a new one and notice how it glistens and for an instant I catch an image of the sky on its soft face. As I place the putty flesh next to the glass, my fingers feel it resist as if it already knew what I planned for it. Hours later I find my daughter touching the pane as if she expected it to tell her something new. Perhaps it did, I never went close enough to find out. I stayed back thinking of her and of my father and of the glass broken suddenly during the night and for a long time I will not be able to go to that window and look out.

BROKEN SHOULDER

Your arm hangs from your broken shoulder and you feel pain
when I come near. I feel the room swell as it fills with our
exhaust. I make up excuses because I know you are not angry.
You look at me and for a moment I think you see our son then I
look away moving my hands to your back. I want to pull
myself in close and breathe you. My tongue is suited for less
graceful work and hesitates when I draw near.

I can see your clothes hanging in the closet across the room and
for a moment they dance with a glimmer of your form. The red
blouse you wore on the day you fell and broke your shoulder
stands out as if it admired itself too much. I want to get up and
close the closet door but don't. I turn to your face instead, still
partly filled with sleep. I move my hands over your breasts as
if it were the first time I had held them. My small hands
tremble and I can feel you quake briefly. Your eyes do not
open and I move my hands lower until I can feel your softest
place. Suddenly your moist folds seem to speak to me and I
want to fill you with my finger but I don't, wait instead while
you begin to move yourself awake. My finger stays long after
you wake and clasp me as if you wanted to pull me in.

But you don't as I move inside with my finger filling your head
your eyes your arms and fingers and still you sway and I listen
not for a given sigh or moan so particular to you but for
something in both of us to erupt something new and
spontaneous.

I replace my finger with my mouth and hold you open lip to lip.
Things begin to pour into this room then. First the moonlight,
then voices, then the city calling us as if we were far away from
it and lost. But they are the strange things our lives try to keep
out. I want to be buried in you, to find your sweetness in my

mouth as I break through the earth for light. We linger within each other until morning brings the usual signs. I wait for you to rise your arm still dangling from its broken socket. You do everything with your right hand. First opening the blinds as if behind them somewhere the world waited to be set in motion. Moving to the mirror you stand alone forgetting for a moment that I am watching, then you turn to me and smile the smile you use only for me. I hold my hand up as if it held a dozen roses or contained the solution to something important. Your eyebrows meet for a moment and I am caught by that and must listen again for spring outside as if it was too large and got wedged between the houses on our block.

Some mornings I wake and feel you brush your lips against my back as if you wanted your kisses to grow there. I lose everything except this room and your mouth. Our children downstairs wait for their lives. I would like to start making love right then, but you rise slowly to get dressed and I can see that longing is necessary. I get up and look across the city. I imagine people in stores downtown feeling much the same way, having left their beds reluctantly.

Tomorrow when I think of our lovemaking I will remember your arm first and how despite the pain you held me for a moment with it. I could feel that its strength was so much less than your good arm and still it held me more completely than I could you.

There can be none, only a short wave or certain smile that comes again when you are asleep or talking to your daughter, her head tossed a particular way as if she were trying to figure you out. On some Saturday or Sunday you will call home and there will be no answer only a long ringing in your ear, and as you put down the receiver the words will form again at the back of your mind, and you will think of a particular colour or taste, and you will open your mouth as if to speak but you will step forward instead and look into your hands as if they held something beautiful, and as you do you will begin to cry, and from across the room a thin pale smoke will drift as if your father has just finished smoking one of his strong cigarettes. You will stare at the empty chair. The house quiet on a quiet street. Off in the distance a dog will bark at someone. The world will become so faint that you will begin to see behind it the face of your father and his eyes. How did they get there?

SMALLNESS

My father is small.
My words are small as they
try to reach him as he sleeps.
Later, I watch his fingers play
in his pants pocket as he stands
across from me and smiles.
He only has two teeth left,
the rest rotting and falling out.
He laughs when I say something silly
and I like that.
My life is small.
When I ask my father a question
he writes something down
and I turn away knowing how small
his writing will be.

Death is small, the way it
opens inside of someone
like the smallest bloom
of the season.
My memory is small and contains
only the voices you have used
when you sing to me at night.
Each space we cross is small
and as you touch me I feel how
beautiful small is.

Nothing is large. Everything is small,
even what God prepares for us
when he has the time.
And when I think about that
I am happy, because being small
is the most important thing there is.
Without knowing that we will never
escape what holds us back.
So when I touch you or come to you
with a flower in my mouth,
think of smallness.